Ninja Dual Zone

Air Fryer Cookbook UK

Easy and Yummy British Recipes for Fast and Healthy Meals with European Measurements and Ingredients

Isaac Reed

Contents

FISH & SEAFOOD RECIPES 41

SNACKS & APPETIZERS RECIPES 47

VEGAN & VEGETARIAN RECIPES 53

VEGETABLE & SIDE DISHES 61

OTHER AIR FRYER RECIPES 67

HOW DOES AN AIR FRYER WORK?

The first think you're probably wondering is how an Air Fryer works. How is it any different than a regular deep fryer or an oven? Most importantly, Air Fryers are different from regular deep fryers because they don't actually fry food, meaning you don't actually submerge your food in hot oil to cook it.

The actual mechanism of Air Fryers is most akin to that of a convection oven. Basically, your food is placed in a perforated metal basket. At the top is a heating unit with a high powered fan that blows the hot air all around the food, creating a convection effect that nicely and evenly browns the outside of the food. And unlike a convection oven, Air Fryers are compact, allowing for faster and more efficient preheating and cooking times.

10 REASONS TO BUY AN AIR FRYER

1) It makes delicious food !

When you bake food in regular ovens (especially not convention ovens), you are often left with uneven results, with some parts burnt and other parts undercooked. The mechanism of Air Fryers described above allows hot air to circulate all around the food, maximizing surface area-to-heat ratio and allowing for perfectly even crispiness and crunchiness. While an Air Fryer won't taste exactly like if you used a traditional deep fryer, we really love the end result of each recipe we've tried so far.

2) It is a healthier option

Love the taste of fried food but not the way it makes you feel afterwards (for instance Zoe tends to get heartburn with fried food)? Are you disappointed with the end result when you try the oven-roasted version of the same recipe? If yes to these questions, then an Air Fryer might be the solution!

You can usually get away with using little-to-no oil when cooking with an Air Fryer, which can cut calories. Furthermore, one study (Sansano et at., 2015) showed that compared to traditional frying methods, using an air fryer reduces acrylamide (a compound associated with certain types of cancer) by up to 90%.

3) It is time and energy efficient

With their compact size and efficient circulation of hot air, Air Fryers out-compete your oven. With most recipes only needing 8-20 minutes of cooking, Air Fryers reduce cooking time by up to 25% (they also only need a fraction of the time to preheat, unlike your oven), saving you both time and energy.

4) There's an air fryer for every price range

With prices as low as $40, buying an Air Fryer doesn't have to break your wallet. We are obviously more than happy with our investment in an Air Fryer. And don't worry, even the lower-priced ones still produce great results! Keep reading this Ultimate Air Fryer Guide to see the specific products we recommend.

5) They are easy to clean

With removable parts, nonstick materials, and most being dishwasher-safe, cleaning your air fryer is no hassle at all! And compared to the grease that coats your kitchen walls after deep frying foods, an Air Fryer produces no mess.

6) They are versatile and can make all kinds of recipes

See below for a sample of all of the different types of food you can make using an Air Fryer. From meat to vegetables to even pizza, we've been able to incorporate air frying into a ton of our meal preparations.

7) Many have different modes, allowing different types of cooking

Not only used for frying foods, an Air Fryer can also be used for reheating leftovers, thawing frozen food, and much, much more. Ours lets you change the settings to "air fry", "roast", "dehydrate", and "reheat". It's up to you to experiment!

8) They come in all different shapes and sizes

It's true that they take up some counter space. But there's an Air Fryer of every size to fit your needs. If you mostly cook for one or two people, you can get away with 2 to 3 quart sized Air Fryers. If you usually cook for a family of 3-5, consider 5 to 6 quart ones. But generally, air fryers between 3 to 5 quarts are versatile enough for most types and quantities of cooking.

9) They make for a great gift

What a perfect gift for the budding home chef?! I got ours for Zoe for Christmas. But whether its for a birthday, wedding registry, or any other special occasion, an Air Fryer makes for an ideal long-lasting and useful present.

10) They let you join the Air Fryer community

With niche Air Fryer blogs to Air Fryer recipe books, buying one of these lets you drastically expand your culinary repertoire and connect with a whole new community of home chefs.

HOW TO USE AN AIR FRYER

The Air Fryer's Versatility

Get ready to challenge everything you know about frying foods. Air fryers can fry your favorite foods to crispy, golden brown perfection (yes, French fries and potato chips!) using little or no oil. Not only can you make traditionally fried foods like potato chips and French fries, but it's also great for vegetables, proteins like chicken wings and drummettes, and appetizers like coquettes and feta triangles. Even desserts like brownies and blondies are perfectly baked in an air fryer.

Why It Works

Put in other terms, an air fryer is much like a convection oven but in a different outfit, cooking food at very high temperatures while simultaneously circulating dry air around the food, cooking food faster all the while making it crisp without needing to add extra fat.

What to Look for in an Air Fryer

There are a lot of different sizes and types of air fryers available now. If you're cooking for a crowd, try an the Philips XXL Air Fryer which can cook an entire chicken or six portions of fries.

If you have limited counter space, try the Philips Avance Air Fryer which uses patented technology to circulate hot air, yielding crunchy, satisfying results. and this next-generation air fryer boasts a more compact size (same capacity!) and TurboStar technology, which ensures food cooks evenly (no more worrying about pile-ups). Now you can enjoy all the fried foods you love—without the guilt.

To up an air fryer's versatility even more, You can also buy a variety of different attachments, such as a rack, grill pan, muffin pans and mesh baskets) to for entertaining. Check out our Air Fryer seasonings that we developed in-house, ranging from Buttermilk Black Pepper Seasoning for air-frying chicken to Garlic Sichuan Seasoning perfect for Chinese cooking.

Read on for a video on the air fryer in action, how-to tips and our favorite recipes, including those fries, air-fried tonkotsu, chicken wings and more.

FIVE TIPS FOR USING AN AIR FRYER

1. Shake it.

Be sure to open the air fryer and shake foods around as they "fry" in the machine's basket—smaller foods like French fries and chips can compress. For best results, rotate them every 5-10 minutes.

2. Don't overcrowd.

Give foods plenty of space so that the air can circulate effectively; that's what gives you crispy results. Our test kitchen cooks swear by the air fryer for snacks and small batches.

3. Give foods a spray.

Lightly spray foods with cooking spray or add just a bit of oil to ensure they don't stick to the basket.

4. Keep it dry.

Pat foods dry before cooking (if they are marinated, for example) to avoid splattering and excess smoke. Similarly, when cooking high-fat foods like chicken wings, make sure to empty the fat from the bottom machine periodically.

5. Master other cooking methods.

The air fryer isn't just for frying; it's great for other healthy cooking methods like baking, roasting and grilling, too. Our test kitchen also loves to use the machine for cooking salmon!

Breakfast & Brunch Recipes

Craving Cinnamon Toast

Servings: 6   Cooking Time: 15 Mins.

>>> Ingredients:

- Pepper to taste
- ½ C. sugar
- 1 stick butter
- 1½ tbsp vanilla extract
- 1½ tbsp cinnamon

>>> Directions:

1. In a microwave-proof bowl, mix butter, pepper, sugar and vanilla extract. Warm and stir the mixture for 30 seconds until everything melts. Pour the mixture over bread slices. Lay the bread slices in your air fryer's cooking basket and cook for 5 Mins. at 400 F. Serve with fresh banana and berry sauce.

Coconut Berries Bowls

Servings: 4   Cooking Time: 15 Mins.

>>> Ingredients:

- 1 and ½ C. coconut milk
- ½ C. blackberries
- 2 tsp. stevia
- ½ C. coconut, shredded

>>> Directions:

1. In your air fryer's pan, mix all the ingredients, stir, cover and cook at 360 degrees F for 15 minutes. Divide into bowls and serve for breakfast.

Savory Carrot Muffins

Servings: 6 Cooking Time: 14 Mins.

>>> Ingredients:

- For Muffins:
- ¼ C. whole-wheat flour
- ¼ C. all-purpose flour
- ½ tsp. baking powder
- 1/8 tsp. baking soda
- ½ tsp. dried parsley, crushed
- ½ tsp. salt
- ½ C. yogurt
- 1 tsp. vinegar
- 1 tbsp. vegetable oil
- 3 tbsp. cottage cheese, grated
- 1 carrot, peeled and grated
- 2-4 tbsp. water (if needed)
- For Topping:
- 7 oz. Parmesan cheese, grated
- ¼ C. walnuts, chopped

>>> Directions:

1. Set the temperature of Air Fryer to 355 degrees F. Grease 6 medium muffin molds.
2. For muffin: in a large bowl, mix together the flours, baking powder, baking soda, parsley, and salt.
3. In another large bowl, mix well the yogurt, and vinegar.
4. Add the remaining ingredients except water and beat them well. (add some water if needed)
5. Make a well in the center of the yogurt mixture.
6. Slowly, add the flour mixture in the well and mix until well combined.
7. Place the mixture evenly into the prepared muffin molds and top with the Parmesan cheese and walnuts.
8. Place the muffin molds into an Air Fryer basket in 2 batches.
9. Air Fry for about 7 Mins. or until a toothpick inserted in the center comes out clean.
10. Remove the muffin molds from Air Fryer and place onto a wire rack to cool for about 10 minutes.
11. Carefully, invert the muffins onto the wire rack to completely cool before serving.
12. Enjoy!

Basil Tomato Bowls

Servings: 4 Cooking Time: 15 Mins.

>>> Ingredients:

- 🌀 1 lb. cherry tomatoes, halved
- 🌀 1 C. mozzarella, shredded
- 🌀 Cooking spray
- 🌀 Salt and black pepper to the taste
- 🌀 1 tsp. basil, chopped

>>> Directions:

1. Grease the tomatoes with the cooking spray, season with salt and pepper, sprinkle the mozzarella on top, place them all in your air fryer's basket, cook at 330 degrees F for 15 minutes, divide into bowls, sprinkle the basil on top and serve.

Simple Egg Soufflé

Servings: 2 Cooking Time: 8 Mins.

>>> Ingredients:

- 🌀 2 eggs
- 🌀 1/4 tsp chili pepper
- 🌀 2 tbsp heavy cream
- 🌀 1/4 tsp pepper
- 🌀 1 tbsp parsley, chopped
- 🌀 Salt

>>> Directions:

1. In a bowl, whisk eggs with remaining gradients.
2. Spray two ramekins with cooking spray.
3. Pour egg mixture into the prepared ramekins and place into the air fryer basket.
4. Cook soufflé at 390 F for 8 minutes.
5. Serve and enjoy.

Strawberry Rhubarb Parfait

Servings: 1 Cooking Time: 1-2 Days

>>> Ingredients:

- 1 package crème fraiche or plain full-fat yogurt (8.5 oz)
- 2 tbsp toasted flakes
- 2 tbsp toasted coconut flakes
- 6 tbsp homemade strawberry and rhubarb jam (4.25 oz)

>>> Directions:

1. Add the jam into a dessert bowl (3 tbsp per serving).
2. Add the crème fraîche and garnish with the toasted and coconut flakes.
3. Serve!

Strawberry Oatmeal

Servings: 4 Cooking Time: 10 Mins.

>>> Ingredients:

- 1 C. strawberries, chopped
- 1 C. steel cut oats
- 1 C. almond milk
- 2 tbsp. sugar
- ½ tsp. vanilla extract
- Cooking spray

>>> Directions:

1. Spray your air fryer with cooking spray and then add all ingredients; toss and cover.
2. Cook at 365 degrees F for 10 minutes.
3. Divide into bowls and serve.

Apple Oatmeal

Servings: 6   Cooking Time: 15 Mins.

>>> Ingredients:

- 3 C. almond milk
- 2 apples, cored, peeled and chopped
- 1¼ C. steel cut oats
- ½ tsp. cinnamon powder
- ¼ tsp. nutmeg, ground
- ¼ tsp. allspice, ground
- ¼ tsp. ginger powder
- ¼ tsp. cardamom, ground
- 2 tsp. vanilla extract
- 2 tsp. sugar
- Cooking spray

>>> Directions:

1. Spray your air fryer with cooking spray, add all ingredients, and stir.
2. Cover and cook at 360 degrees F for 15 minutes.
3. Divide into bowls and serve.

Lunch & Dinner Recipes

Potato Croquettes

Servings: 10   Cooking Time: 25 Mins.

>>> Ingredients:

- ¼ C. nutritional yeast
- 2 C. boiled potatoes, mashed
- 1 flax egg [1 tbsp. flaxseed meal + 3 tbsp. water]
- 1 tbsp. flour
- 2 tbsp. chives, chopped
- Salt and pepper to taste
- 2 tbsp. vegetable oil
- ¼ C. bread crumbs

>>> Directions:

1. Pre-heat the Air Fryer to 400°F.
2. In a bowl, combine together the nutritional yeast, potatoes, flax eggs, flour, and chives. Sprinkle with salt and pepper as desired.
3. In separate bowl mix together the vegetable oil and bread crumbs to achieve a crumbly consistency.
4. Use your hands to shape the potato mixture into small balls and dip each one into the breadcrumb mixture.
5. Place the croquettes inside the air fryer and cook for 15 minutes, ensuring the croquettes turn golden brown.

Paprika Tofu

Servings: 4   Cooking Time: 25 Mins.

>>> Ingredients:

- 2 block extra firm tofu, pressed to remove excess water and cubed
- ¼ C. cornstarch
- 1 tbsp. smoked paprika
- Salt and pepper to taste

>>> Directions:

1. Cover the Air Fryer basket with aluminum foil and coat with a light brushing of oil.
2. Pre-heat the Air Fryer to 370°F.
3. Combine all ingredients in a bowl, coating the tofu well.
4. Put in the Air Fryer basket and allow to cook for 12 minutes.

Herbed Butter Beef Loin

>>> Ingredients:

- 1 tbsp. butter, melted
- ¼ dried thyme
- 1 tsp. garlic salt
- ¼ tsp. dried parsley
- 1 lb. beef loin

>>> Directions:

1. In a bowl, combine the melted butter, thyme, garlic salt, and parsley.
2. Cut the beef loin into slices and generously apply the seasoned butter using a brush.
3. Pre-heat your fryer at 400°F and place a rack inside.
4. Cook the beef for fifteen minutes.
5. Take care when removing it and serve hot.

Amazing Beef Stew

>>> Ingredients:

- 2 lbs. beef meat; cut into medium chunks
- 2 carrots; chopped
- 4 potatoes; chopped
- 1-quart veggie stock
- 1/2 tsp. smoked paprika
- A handful thyme; chopped
- Salt and black pepper to the taste

>>> Directions:

1. In a dish that fits your air fryer; mix beef with carrots, potatoes, stock, salt, pepper, paprika and thyme; stir, place in air fryer's basket and cook at 375 °F, for 20 minutes. Divide into bowls and serve right away for lunch.

Shrimp Salad

Servings: 4

Cooking Time: 3 Mins.

>>> Ingredients:

- 1-pound shrimps, peeled
- 1 tbsp. lemon juice
- ½ tsp. ground cardamom
- ¼ tsp. salt
- ½ tsp. ground paprika
- 1 tbsp. olive oil
- 1 garlic clove, diced
- 1 avocado, peeled, pitted, chopped
- 1 tsp. chives, chopped

>>> Directions:

1. Put the shrimps in the big bowl. Add lemon juice, ground nutmeg, salt, and ground paprika. Mix up the shrimps and leave them for 10 Mins. to marinate. Meanwhile, preheat the air fryer to 400F. Put the marinated shrimps in the air fryer and cook them for 3 minutes. It is recommended to arrange shrimps in one layer. Meanwhile, put the chopped avocado in the bowl and sprinkle it with diced garlic and chives. Cool the shrimps to the room temperature and add in the avocado bowl. Sprinkle the salad with olive oil. After this, gently mix the salad with the help of two spoons.

Sriracha Cauliflower

>>> Ingredients:

- ¼ C. vegan butter, melted
- ¼ C. sriracha sauce
- 4 C. cauliflower florets
- 1 C. bread crumbs
- 1 tsp. salt

>>> Directions:

1. Mix together the sriracha and vegan butter in a bowl and pour this mixture over the cauliflower, taking care to cover each floret entirely.
2. In a separate bowl, combine the bread crumbs and salt.
3. Dip the cauliflower florets in the bread crumbs, coating each one well. Cook in the Air Fryer for 17 Mins. in a 375°F pre-heated Air Fryer.

Broccoli Salad

>>> Ingredients:

- 1 C. broccoli florets
- 1 tsp. olive oil
- 1 tbsp. hazelnuts, chopped
- 4 bacon slices
- ½ tsp. salt
- ½ tsp. lemon zest, grated
- ½ tsp. sesame oil

>>> Directions:

1. Mix up broccoli florets with olive oil, salt, and lemon zest. Shake the vegetables well. Preheat the air fryer to 385F. Put the broccoli in the air fryer basket and cook for 8 minutes. Shake the broccoli after 4 Mins. of cooking. Then transfer the broccoli in the salad bowl. Place the bacon in the air fryer and cook it at 400F for 10 Mins. or until it is crunchy. Chop the cooked bacon and add in the broccoli. After this, add hazelnuts and sesame oil. Stir the salad gently.

Pasta Salad

Servings: 8

Cooking Time: 2 Hours 25 Mins.

>>> Ingredients:

- 4 tomatoes, medium and cut in eighths
- 3 eggplants, small
- 3 zucchinis, medium sized
- 2 bell peppers, any color
- 4 C. large pasta, uncooked in any shape
- 1 C. cherry tomatoes, sliced
- ½ C. Italian dressing, fat-free
- 8 tbsp. parmesan, grated
- 2 tbsp. extra virgin olive oil
- 2 tsp. pink Himalayan salt
- 1 tsp. basil, dried
- High quality cooking spray

>>> Directions:

1. Wash and dry the eggplant. Cut off the stem and throw it away. Do not peel the eggplant. Cut it into half-inch-thick round slices.
2. Coat the eggplant slices with 1 tbsp. of extra virgin olive oil, and transfer to the Air Fryer basket.
3. Cook the eggplant for 40 Mins. at 350°F. Once it is tender and cooked through, remove from the fryer and set to one side.
4. Wash and dry the zucchini. Cut off the stem and throw it away. Do not peel the zucchini. Cut the zucchini into half-inch-thick round slices.
5. Combine with the olive oil to coat, and put it in the Air Fryer basket.
6. Cook the zucchini for about 25 Mins. at 350°F. Once it is tender and cooked through, remove from the fryer and set to one side.
7. Wash the tomatoes and cut them into eight equal slices. Transfer them to the fryer basket and spritz lightly with high quality cooking spray. Cook the tomatoes for 30 Mins. at 350°F. Once they have shrunk and are beginning to turn brown, set them to one side.
8. Cook the pasta and drain it. Rinse with cold water and set it aside to cool.
9. Wash, dry and halve the bell peppers. Remove the stems and seeds.
10. Wash and halve the cherry tomatoes.
11. In a large bowl, mix together the bell peppers and cherry tomatoes. Stir in the roasted vegetables, cooked pasta, pink Himalayan salt, dressing, chopped basil leaves, and grated parmesan, ensuring to incorporate everything well.
12. Let the salad cool and marinate in the refrigerator.
13. Serve the salad cold or at room temperature.

Desserts Recipes

Vanilla Bean Dream

>>> Ingredients:

- ½ C. extra virgin coconut oil, softened
- ½ C. coconut butter, softened
- Juice of 1 lemon
- Seeds from ½ a vanilla bean

>>> Directions:

1. Whisk the ingredients in an easy-to-pour cup.
2. Pour into a lined cupcake or loaf pan.
3. Refrigerate for 20 minutes. Top with lemon zest.
4. Serve!

Lemon Butter Bars

>>> Ingredients:

- ½ C. butter, melted
- 1 C. erythritol
- 1 and ¾ C. almond flour
- 3 eggs, whisked
- Zest of 1 lemon, grated
- Juice of 3 lemons

>>> Directions:

1. In a bowl, mix 1 C. flour with half of the erythritol and the butter, stir well and press into a baking dish that fits the air fryer lined with parchment paper. Put the dish in your air fryer and cook at 350 degrees F for 10 minutes. Meanwhile, in a bowl, mix the rest of the flour with the remaining erythritol and the other ingredients and whisk well. Spread this over the crust, put the dish in the air fryer once more and cook at 350 degrees F for 25 minutes. Cool down, cut into bars and serve.

Mint Cake

Servings: 2

Cooking Time: 9 Mins.

>>> Ingredients:

- 1 tbsp. cocoa powder
- 2 tbsp. coconut oil, softened
- 2 tbsp. Erythritol
- 1 tsp. peppermint
- 3 eggs, beaten
- 1 tsp. spearmint, dried
- 4 tsp. almond flour
- Cooking spray

>>> Directions:

1. Preheat the air fryer to 375F. Melt the coconut oil in the microwave oven for 10 seconds. Then add cocoa powder and almond flour in the melted coconut oil. After this, add Erythritol, peppermint, and spearmint. Add eggs and whisk the mixture until smooth. Spray the ramekins with cooking spray and pour the chocolate mixture inside. Then put the ramekins with lava cakes in the preheated air fryer and cook them for 9 minutes. Then remove the cooked lava cakes from the air fryer and let them rest for 5 Mins. before serving.

Milky Doughnuts

>>> Ingredients:

- For Doughnuts:
- 1 C. all-purpose flour
- 1 C. whole wheat flour
- 2 tsp. baking powder
- Salt, to taste
- ¾ C. sugar
- 1 egg
- 1 tbsp. butter, softened
- ½ C. milk
- 2 tsp. vanilla extract
- For Glaze:
- 2 tbsp. icing sugar
- 2 tbsp. condensed milk
- 1 tbsp. cocoa powder

>>> Directions:

1. In a large bowl, mix well flours, baking powder, and salt.
2. In another bowl, add the sugar and egg. Whisk until fluffy and light.
3. Add the flour mixture and stir until well combined.
4. Add the butter, milk, and vanilla extract and mix until a soft dough forms.
5. Refrigerate the dough for at least 1 hour.
6. Now, put the dough onto a lightly floured surface and roll into ½-inch thickness.
7. With a small doughnut cutter, cut 24 small doughnuts from the rolled dough.
8. Set the temperature of air fryer to 390 degrees F. Grease an air fryer basket.
9. Place doughnuts into the prepared air fryer basket in 3 batches.
10. Air fry for about 6-8 minutes.
11. Remove from air fryer and transfer the doughnuts onto a platter to cool completely.
12. In a small bowl, mix together the condensed milk and cocoa powder.
13. Spread the glaze over doughnuts and sprinkle with icing sugar.
14. Serve.

Butter Custard

>>> Ingredients:

- ¼ C. heavy cream
- 1 tbsp. Erythritol
- 1 tsp. coconut flour
- 3 egg yolks
- 1 tsp. butter

>>> Directions:

1. Whip the heavy cream and them mix it up with Erythritol and coconut flour. Whisk the egg yolks and add them in the whipped cream mixture. Then grease 2 ramekins with butter and transfer the whipped cream mixture in the ramekins. Preheat the air fryer to 300F. Put the ramekins with custard in the air fryer and cook them for 35 minutes.

Cream Cheese Muffins

>>> Ingredients:

- 2 eggs
- 1/2 C. erythritol
- 8 oz cream cheese
- 1 tsp ground cinnamon
- 1/2 tsp vanilla

>>> Directions:

1. Preheat the air fryer to 325 F.
2. In a bowl, mix together cream cheese, vanilla, erythritol, and eggs until soft.
3. Pour batter into the silicone muffin molds and sprinkle cinnamon on top.
4. Place muffin molds into the air fryer basket and cook for 16 minutes.
5. Serve and enjoy.

Doughnuts Pudding

>>> Ingredients:

- 6 glazed doughnuts, cut into small pieces
- ¾ C. frozen sweet cherries
- ½ C. raisins
- ½ C. semi-sweet chocolate baking chips
- 4 egg yolks
- ¼ C. sugar
- 1 tsp. ground cinnamon
- 1½ C. whipping cream

>>> Directions:

1. Preheat the Air fryer to 310F and grease a baking dish lightly.
2. Mix doughnut pieces, cherries, raisins, chocolate chips, sugar, and cinnamon in a large bowl.
3. Whisk the egg yolks with whipping cream in another bowl until well combined.
4. Combine the egg yolk mixture into the doughnut mixture and mix well.
5. Arrange the doughnuts mixture evenly into the baking dish and transfer into the Air fryer basket.
6. Cook for about 60 Mins. and dish out to serve warm.

Strawberry Pop Tarts

Servings: 6

Cooking Time: 25 Mins.

>>> Ingredients:

- 1 oz reduced-fat Philadelphia cream cheese
- 1 tsp cornstarch
- 1 tsp stevia
- 1 tsp sugar sprinkles
- 1/2 C. plain, non-fat vanilla Greek yogurt
- 1/3 C. low-sugar strawberry preserves
- 2 refrigerated pie crusts
- olive oil or coconut oil spray

>>> Directions:

1. Cut pie crusts into 6 equal rectangles.
2. In a bowl, mix cornstarch and preserves. Add preserves in middle of crust. Fold over crust. Crimp edges with fork to seal. Repeat process for remaining crusts.
3. Lightly grease baking pan of air fryer with cooking spray. Add pop tarts in single layer. Cook in batches for 8 Mins. at 370oF.
4. Meanwhile, make the frosting by mixing stevia, cream cheese, and yogurt in a bowl. Spread on top of cooked pop tart and add sugar sprinkles.
5. Serve and enjoy.

Poultry Recipes

Thanksgiving Turkey With Mustard Gravy

Servings: 6   Cooking Time: 50 Mins.

>>> Ingredients:

- 2 tsp. butter, softened
- 1 tsp. dried sage
- 2 sprigs rosemary, chopped
- 1 tsp. salt
- 1/4 tsp. freshly ground black pepper, or more to taste
- 1 whole turkey breast
- 2 tbsp. turkey broth
- 2 tbsp. whole-grain mustard
- 1 tbsp. butter

>>> Directions:

1. Start by preheating your Air Fryer to 360 degrees F.
2. To make the rub, combine 2 tbsp. of butter, sage, rosemary, salt, and pepper; mix well to combine and spread it evenly over the surface of the turkey breast.
3. Roast for 20 Mins. in an Air Fryer cooking basket. Flip the turkey breast over and cook for a further 15 to 16 minutes. Now, flip it back over and roast for 12 Mins. more.
4. While the turkey is roasting, whisk the other ingredients in a saucepan. After that, spread the gravy all over the turkey breast.
5. Let the turkey rest for a few Mins. before carving. Bon appétit!

Easy Fried Chicken Southern Style

Servings: 6   Cooking Time: 30 Mins.

>>> Ingredients:

- 1 C. coconut flour
- 1 tsp. garlic powder
- 1 tsp. paprika
- 1 tsp. pepper
- 1 tsp. salt
- 5 lb. chicken leg quarters

>>> Directions:

1. Preheat the air fryer for 5 minutes.
2. Combine all ingredients in a bowl. Give a good stir.
3. Place ingredients in the air fryer.
4. Cook for 30 Mins. at 3500F.

Sage & Onion Turkey Balls

Servings: 2   Cooking Time: 40 Mins.

>>> Ingredients:

- 3.5 oz. turkey mince
- ½ small onion, diced
- 1 medium egg
- 1 tsp. sage
- ½ tsp. garlic, pureed
- 3 tbsp. friendly bread crumbs
- Salt to taste
- Pepper to taste

>>> Directions:

1. Put all of the ingredients in a bowl and mix together well.
2. Take equal portions of the mixture and mold each one into a small ball. Transfer to the Air Fryer and cook for 15 Mins. at 350°F.
3. Serve with tartar sauce and mashed potatoes.

Piri Piri Chicken

Servings: 6 Cooking Time: 1 Hour 30 Mins.

>>> Ingredients:

- 12 chicken wings
- 1 ½ oz. butter, melted
- 1 tsp. onion powder
- 1/2 tsp. cumin powder
- 1 tsp. garlic paste
- For the Sauce:
- 2 oz. piri piri peppers, stemmed and chopped
- 1 tbsp. pimiento, deveined and minced
- 1 garlic clove, chopped
- 2 tbsp. fresh lemon juice
- 1/3 tsp. sea salt
- 1/2 tsp. tarragon

>>> Directions:

1. Steam the chicken wings using a steamer basket that is placed over a saucepan with boiling water; reduce the heat.
2. Now, steam the wings for 10 Mins. over a moderate heat. Toss the wings with butter, onion powder, cumin powder, and garlic paste.
3. Let the chicken wings cool to room temperature. Then, refrigerate them for 45 to 50 minutes.
4. Roast in the preheated Air Fryer at 330 degrees F for 25 to 30 minutes; make sure to flip them halfway through.
5. While the chicken wings are cooking, prepare the sauce by mixing all of the sauce ingredients in a food processor. Toss the wings with prepared Piri Piri Sauce and serve.

Cilantro Lime Chicken

>>> Ingredients:

- 2 lbs chicken thighs, boneless
- 2 tbsp fresh cilantro, chopped
- 1 tsp Montreal chicken seasoning
- 1 tsp soy sauce
- 1/2 lime juice
- 1 tsp olive oil
- Pepper
- Salt

>>> Directions:

1. Whisk together cilantro, seasoning, soy sauce, lime juice, olive oil, pepper, and salt in a large bowl.
2. Add chicken into the bowl and coat well with marinade and place in the refrigerator for overnight.
3. Spray air fryer basket with cooking spray.
4. Place marinated chicken into the air fryer basket and cook at 400 F for 10 minutes.
5. Turn chicken to another side and cook for 10 Mins. more.
6. Serve and enjoy.

Bleu Cheese Chicken Mix

>>> Ingredients:

- 1 lb. chicken breasts, skinless, boneless and cut into thin strips
- 1 small yellow onion, sliced
- ½ C. buffalo sauce
- ½ C. chicken stock
- ¼ C. bleu cheese, crumbled

>>> Directions:

1. In a pan that fits your air fryer, mix the chicken with the onions, buffalo sauce, and the stock.
2. Toss everything and then place the pan in the fryer; cook at 370 degrees F for 20 minutes.
3. Sprinkle the cheese on top, divide everything between plates, and serve.

Stuffed Chicken

>>> Ingredients:

- 8 oz chicken fillet
- 3 oz Blue cheese
- ½ tsp. salt
- ½ tsp. thyme
- 1 tsp. sesame oil

>>> Directions:

1. Cut the fillet into halves and beat them gently with the help of the kitchen hammer. After this, make the horizontal cut in every fillet. Sprinkle the chicken with salt and thyme. Then fill it with Blue cheese and secure the cut with the help of the toothpick. Sprinkle the stuffed chicken fillets with sesame oil. Preheat the air fryer to 385F. Put the chicken fillets in the air fryer and cook them for 7 minutes. Then carefully flip the chicken fillets on another side and cook for 4 Mins. more.

Chicken Burgers

>>> Ingredients:

- ½ onion, chopped
- 2 garlic cloves, chopped
- 1 egg, beaten
- ½ C. breadcrumbs
- ½ tbsp ground cumin
- ½ tbsp paprika
- ½ tbsp cilantro seeds, crushed
- Salt and pepper to taste

>>> Directions:

1. In a bowl, mix chicken, onion, garlic, egg, breadcrumbs, cumin, paprika, cilantro, salt, and black pepper, with hands; shape into 4 patties. Grease the air fryer with oil, and arrange the patties inside. Do not layer them. Cook in batches if needed. Cook for 10 Mins. at 380 F, turning once halfway through.

Beef,pork & Lamb Recipes

Peppery Pork Roast With Herbs

>>> Ingredients:

- 1 tbsp. olive oil
- 1 lb. pork loin
- 1 tsp. dried basil
- 1/2 tsp. dried oregano
- 1/4 tsp. crushed red pepper flakes
- 1 tsp. dried thyme
- 1/4 tsp. freshly grated nutmeg
- Sea salt flakes and freshly ground black pepper, to taste
- 1 Pimento chili pepper, deveined and chopped
- 1 Yellow wax pepper, deveined and chopped
- 1 bell pepper, deveined and chopped
- 1 tbsp. peanut butter
- 1/4 C. beef broth
- 1/2 tbsp. whole-grain mustard
- 1 bay leaf

>>> Directions:

1. Lightly grease the inside of an Air Fryer baking dish with a thin layer of olive oil. Then, cut 8 slit down the center of pork (about 3x3"). Sprinkle with the seasonings and massage them into the meat to evenly distribute

2. Then, tuck peppers into the slits and transfer the meat to the Air Fryer baking dish. Scatter remaining peppers around the roast.

3. In a mixing dish, whisk the peanut butter, beef broth, and mustard; now, pour broth mixture around the roast.

4. Add the bay leaf and roast the meat for 25 Mins. at 390 degrees F; turn the pork over halfway through the roasting time. Bon appétit!

Meatballs'n Parmesan-cheddar Pizza

Servings: 4
Cooking Time: 15 Mins.

>>> Ingredients:

- 1 prebaked 6-inch pizza crust
- 1 tsp. garlic powder
- 1 tsp. Italian seasoning
- 4 tbsp grated Parmesan cheese
- 1 small onion, halved and sliced
- 1/2 can (8 ounces) pizza sauce
- 6 frozen fully cooked Italian meatballs (1/2 oz. each), thawed and halved
- 1/2 C. shredded part-skim mozzarella cheese
- 1/2 C. shredded cheddar cheese

>>> Directions:

1. Lightly grease baking pan of air fryer with cooking spray.
2. Place crust on bottom of pan. Spread sauce on top. Sprinkle with parmesan, Italian seasoning, and garlic powder.
3. Top with meatballs and onion. Sprinkle remaining cheese.
4. For 15 minutes, cook on preheated 390oF air fryer.
5. Serve and enjoy.

Greek Lamb Chops

>>> Ingredients:

- 4 lamb chops
- 1 tbsp. white flour
- 2 tbsp. olive oil
- Salt and black pepper to taste
- 1 tsp. marjoram, dried
- 3 garlic cloves, minced
- 1 tsp. thyme, dried
- ½ C. veggie stock
- 1 C. green olives, pitted and sliced

>>> Directions:

1. Place all ingredients—except the olives—in a bowl and mix well. Then put in the fridge for 10 minutes.
2. Transfer the lamb chops to your air fryer's basket and cook at 390 degrees F for 7 Mins. on each side.
3. Divide the lamb chops between plates, sprinkle the olives on top, and serve.

Classic Smoked Pork Chops

>>> Ingredients:

- 6 pork chops
- Hickory-smoked salt, to savor
- Ground black pepper, to savor
- 1 tsp. onion powder
- 1/2 tsp. garlic powder
- 1/2 tsp. cayenne pepper
- 1/3 C. almond meal

>>> Directions:

1. Simply place all of the above ingredients into a zip-top plastic bag; shake them up to coat well.
2. Spritz the chops with a pan spray (canola spray works well here) and transfer them to the Air Fryer cooking basket.
3. Roast them for 20 Mins. at 375 degrees F. Serve with sautéed vegetables. Bon appétit!

Must-serve Cajun Beef Tenderloin

>>> Ingredients:

- 1/3 C. beef broth
- 2 tbsp. Cajun seasoning, crushed
- 1/2 tsp. garlic powder
- 7 oz. beef tenderloins
- ½ tbsp. pear cider vinegar
- 1/3 tsp. cayenne pepper
- 1 ½ tbsp. olive oil
- 1/2 tsp. freshly ground black pepper
- 1 tsp. salt

>>> Directions:

1. Firstly, coat the beef tenderloins with salt, cayenne pepper, and black pepper.
2. Mix the remaining items in a medium-sized bowl; let the meat marinate for 40 Mins. in this mixture.
3. Roast the beef for about 22 Mins. at 385 degrees F, turning it halfway through the cooking time. Bon appétit!

Champagne-vinegar Marinated Skirt Steak

>>> Ingredients:

- ¼ C. Dijon mustard
- 1 tbsp. rosemary leaves
- 1-pound skirt steak, trimmed
- 2 tbsp. champagne vinegar
- Salt and pepper to taste

>>> Directions:

1. Place all ingredients in a Ziploc bag and marinate in the fridge for 2 hours.
2. Preheat the air fryer to 3900F.
3. Place the grill pan accessory in the air fryer.
4. Grill the skirt steak for 20 Mins. per batch.
5. Flip the beef halfway through the cooking time.

Grilled Tri Tip Over Beet Salad

Servings: 6   Cooking Time: 45 Mins.

>>> Ingredients:

- 1 bunch arugula, torn
- 1 bunch scallions, chopped
- 1-pound tri-tip, sliced
- 2 tbsp. olive oil
- 3 beets, peeled and sliced thinly
- 3 tbsp. balsamic vinegar
- Salt and pepper to taste

>>> Directions:

1. Preheat the air fryer to 3900F.
2. Place the grill pan accessory in the air fryer.
3. Season the tri-tip with salt and pepper. Drizzle with oil.
4. Grill for 15 Mins. per batch.
5. Meanwhile, prepare the salad by tossing the rest of the ingredients in a salad bowl.
6. Toss in the grilled tri-trip and drizzle with more balsamic vinegar.

Pork And Garlic Sauce

Servings: 4   Cooking Time: 25 Mins.

>>> Ingredients:

- 1 lb. pork tenderloin, sliced
- A pinch of salt and black pepper
- 4 tbsp. butter, melted
- 2 tsp. garlic, minced
- 1 tsp. sweet paprika

>>> Directions:

1. Heat up a pan that fits the air fryer with the butter over medium heat, add all the ingredients except the pork medallions, whisk well and simmer for 4-5 minutes. Add the pork, toss, put the pan in your air fryer and cook at 380 degrees F for 20 minutes. Divide between plates and serve with a side salad.

Fish & Seafood Recipes

Air Fried Calamari

Servings: 3 Cooking Time: 30 Mins.

>>> Ingredients:

- ½ C. cornmeal or cornstarch
- 2 large eggs, beaten
- 2 mashed garlic cloves
- 1 C. breadcrumbs
- lemon juice

>>> Directions:

1. Coat calamari with the cornmeal. The first mixture is prepared by mixing the eggs and garlic. Dip the calamari in the eggs' mixture. Then dip them in the breadcrumbs. Put the rings in the fridge for 2 hours.
2. Then, line them in the air fryer and add oil generously. Fry for 10 to 13 Mins. at 390 F, shaking once halfway through. Serve with garlic mayonnaise and top with lemon juice.

Tempting Seafood Platter With Shell Pasta

Servings: 4 Cooking Time: 18 Mins.

>>> Ingredients:

- 14-ounce shell pasta
- 4 (4-ounce) salmon steaks
- ½ lb. cherry tomatoes, halved
- 8 large prawns, peeled and deveined
- 2 tbsp. fresh thyme, chopped
- 4 tbsp. pesto, divided
- 2 tbsp. olive oil
- 2 tbsp. fresh lemon juice

>>> Directions:

1. Preheat the Air fryer to 390F and grease a baking dish.
2. Cook pasta in a large pan of salted water for about 10 minutes.
3. Meanwhile, spread pesto in the bottom of a baking dish.
4. Arrange salmon steaks and cherry tomatoes over pesto and drizzle evenly with olive oil.
5. Top with prawns and sprinkle with lemon juice and thyme.
6. Transfer the baking dish in the Air fryer and cook for about 8 minutes.
7. Serve the seafood mixture with pasta and enjoy.

Shrimp And Sausage Gumbo

Servings: 4   Cooking Time: 12 Mins.

>>> Ingredients:

- 10 oz shrimps, peeled
- 5 oz smoked sausages, chopped
- 1 tsp. olive oil
- 1 tsp. ground black pepper
- 3 spring onions, diced
- 1 jalapeno pepper, chopped
- ½ C. chicken broth
- 1 tsp. chili flakes
- ½ tsp. dried cilantro
- ½ tsp. salt

>>> Directions:

1. Preheat the air fryer to 400F. In the mixing bowl mix up smoked sausages, ground black pepper, and chili flakes. Put the smoked sausages in the air fryer and cook them for 4 minutes. Meanwhile, in the mixing bowl mix up onion, jalapeno pepper, and salt. Put the ingredients in the air fryer baking pan and sprinkle with olive oil. After this, remove the sausages from the air fryer. Put the pan with onion in the air fryer and cook it for 2 minutes. After this, add smoked sausages, dried cilantro, and shrimps. Add chicken broth. Stir the ingredients gently and cook the meal for 6 Mins. at 400F.

Tuna Patties With Cheese Sauce

Servings: 4 Cooking Time: 2 Hours 20 Mins.

>>> Ingredients:

- 1 lb. canned tuna, drained
- 1 egg, whisked
- 1 garlic clove, minced
- 2 tbsp. shallots, minced
- 1 C. Romano cheese, grated
- Sea salt and ground black pepper, to taste
- 1 tbsp. sesame oil
- Cheese Sauce:
- 1 tbsp. butter
- 1 C. beer
- 2 tbsp. Colby cheese, grated

>>> Directions:

1. In a mixing bowl, thoroughly combine the tuna, egg, garlic, shallots, Romano cheese, salt, and black pepper. Shape the tuna mixture into four patties and place in your refrigerator for 2 hours.
2. Brush the patties with sesame oil on both sides. Cook in the preheated Air Fryer at 360 degrees F for 14 minutes.
3. In the meantime, melt the butter in a pan over a moderate heat. Add the beer and whisk until it starts bubbling.
4. Now, stir in the grated cheese and cook for 3 to 4 Mins. longer or until the cheese has melted. Spoon the sauce over the fish cake burgers and serve immediately.

Stevia Cod

Servings: 4   Cooking Time: 14 Mins.

>>> Ingredients:

- 1/3 C. stevia
- 2 tbsp. coconut aminos
- 4 cod fillets, boneless
- A pinch of salt and black pepper

>>> Directions:

1. In a pan that fits the air fryer, combine all the ingredients and toss gently. Introduce the pan in the fryer and cook at 350 degrees F for 14 minutes, flipping the fish halfway. Divide everything between plates and serve.

Tarragon Sea Bass And Risotto

Servings: 4   Cooking Time: 25 Mins.

>>> Ingredients:

- 4 sea bass fillets, boneless
- A pinch of salt and black pepper
- 1 tbsp. ghee, melted
- 1 garlic clove, minced
- 1 C. cauliflower rice
- ½ C. chicken stock
- 1 tbsp. parmesan, grated
- 1 tbsp. chervil, chopped
- 1 tbsp. parsley, chopped
- 1 tbsp. tarragon, chopped

>>> Directions:

1. In a pan that fits your air fryer, mix the cauliflower rice with the stock, parmesan, chervil, tarragon and parsley, toss, introduce the pan in the air fryer and cook at 380 degrees F for 12 minutes. In a bowl, mix the fish with salt, pepper, garlic and melted ghee and toss gently. Put the fish over the cauliflower rice, cook at 380 degrees F for 12 Mins. more, divide everything between plates and serve.

Easy Lobster Tails

Servings: 5 Cooking Time: 20 Mins.

>>> Ingredients:

- 2 lb. fresh lobster tails, cleaned and halved, in shells
- 2 tbsp. butter, melted
- 1 tsp. onion powder
- 1 tsp. cayenne pepper
- Salt and ground black pepper, to taste
- 2 garlic cloves, minced
- 1 C. cornmeal
- 1 C. green olives

>>> Directions:

1. In a plastic closeable bag, thoroughly combine all ingredients; shake to combine well.
2. Transfer the coated lobster tails to the greased cooking basket.
3. Cook in the preheated Air Fryer at 390 degrees for 6 to 7 minutes, shaking the basket halfway through. Work in batches.
4. Serve with green olives and enjoy!

Lemony Tuna

Servings: 8 Cooking Time: 12 Mins.

>>> Ingredients:

- 4 tbsp. fresh parsley, chopped
- 4 (6-ounce) cans water packed plain tuna
- 1 C. breadcrumbs
- 2 eggs
- 4 tsp. Dijon mustard
- 2 tbsp. fresh lime juice
- 6 tbsp. canola oil
- Dash of hot sauce
- Salt and black pepper, to taste

>>> Directions:

1. Preheat the Air fryer to 360F and grease an Air fryer basket.
2. Mix tuna fish, breadcrumbs, mustard, parsley, hot sauce, canola oil, eggs, salt and lime juice in a large bowl.
3. Make equal-sized patties from the mixture and refrigerate for about 3 hours.
4. Transfer the patties into the Air fryer basket and cook for about 12 minutes.
5. Dish out and serve warm.

Snacks & Appetizers Recipes

Saucy Asian Short Ribs

Servings: 4   Cooking Time: 35 Mins.

>>> Ingredients:

- 1 lb. meaty short ribs
- 1/2 rice vinegar
- 2 tbsp. soy sauce
- 1 tbsp. Sriracha sauce
- 2 garlic cloves, minced
- 1 tbsp. daenjang (soybean paste)
- 1 tsp. kochukaru (chili pepper flakes)
- Sea salt and ground black pepper, to taste
- 1 tbsp. sesame oil
- 1/4 C. green onions, roughly chopped

>>> Directions:

1. Place the short ribs, vinegar, soy sauce, Sriracha, garlic, and spices in Ziploc bag; let it marinate overnight.
2. Rub the sides and bottom of the Air Fryer basket with sesame oil. Discard the marinade and transfer the ribs to the prepared cooking basket.
3. Cook the marinated ribs in the preheated Air Fryer at 365 degrees for 17 minutes. Turn the ribs over, brush with the reserved marinade, and cook an additional 15 minutes.
4. Garnish with green onions. Bon appétit!

Roasted Peanuts

Servings: 10   Cooking Time: 14 Mins.

>>> Ingredients:

- 2½ C. raw peanuts
- 1 tbsp. olive oil
- Salt, as required

>>> Directions:

1. Set the temperature of Air Fryer to 320 degrees F.
2. Add the peanuts in an Air Fryer basket in a single layer.
3. Air Fry for about 9 minutes, tossing twice.
4. Remove the peanuts from Air Fryer basket and transfer into a bowl.
5. Add the oil, and salt and toss to coat well.
6. Return the nuts mixture into Air Fryer basket.
7. Air Fry for about 5 minutes.
8. Once done, transfer the hot nuts in a glass or steel bowl and serve.

Chaffle

Servings: 10   Cooking Time: 14 Mins.

>>> Ingredients:

- 4 eggs, beaten
- 2 oz bacon, chopped, cooked
- 1 cucumber, pickled, grated
- 2 oz Cheddar cheese, shredded
- ¼ tsp. salt
- ½ tsp. ground black pepper
- Cooking spray

>>> Directions:

1. In the mixing bowl mix up eggs, bacon, pickled cucumber, cheese, salt, and ground black pepper. Whisk the mixture gently. The chaffle batter is cooked. Then spray the air fryer pan with cooking spray. Pour ¼ part of the liquid inside. Preheat the air fryer to 400F. Put the pan with chaffle in the air fryer basket and cook it for 6 minutes. Then transfer the cooked chaffle in the plate. Repeat the same steps with the remaining chaffle batter. In the end, you should get 4 chaffles.

Almond Coconut Granola

Servings: 4 Cooking Time: 12 Mins.

>>> Ingredients:

- 1 tsp. monk fruit
- 1 tsp. almond butter
- 1 tsp. coconut oil
- 2 tbsp. almonds, chopped
- 1 tsp. pumpkin puree
- ½ tsp. pumpkin pie spices
- 2 tbsp. coconut flakes
- 2 tbsp. pumpkin seeds, crushed
- 1 tsp. hemp seeds
- 1 tsp. flax seeds
- Cooking spray

>>> Directions:

1. In the big bowl mix up almond butter and coconut oil. Microwave the mixture until it is melted. After this, in the separated bowl mix up monk fruit, pumpkin spices, coconut flakes, pumpkin seeds, hemp seeds, and flax seeds. Add the melted coconut oil and pumpkin puree. Then stir the mixture until it is homogenous. Preheat the air fryer to 350F. Then put the pumpkin mixture on the baking paper and make the shape of the square. After this, cut the square on the serving bars and transfer in the preheated air fryer. Cook the pumpkin granola for 12 minutes.

Crispy Shrimps

Servings: 2 Cooking Time: 8 Mins.

>>> Ingredients:

- 1 egg
- ¼ lb. nacho chips, crushed
- 10 shrimps, peeled and deveined
- 1 tbsp. olive oil
- Salt and black pepper, to taste

>>> Directions:

1. Preheat the Air fryer to 365F and grease an Air fryer basket.
2. Crack egg in a shallow dish and beat well.
3. Place the nacho chips in another shallow dish.
4. Season the shrimps with salt and black pepper, coat into egg and then roll into nacho chips.
5. Place the coated shrimps into the Air fryer basket and cook for about 8 minutes.
6. Dish out and serve warm.

Cashew Dip

Servings: 6   Cooking Time: 8 Mins.

>>> Ingredients:

- ½ C. cashews, soaked in water for 4 hours and drained
- 3 tbsp. cilantro, chopped
- 2 garlic cloves, minced
- 1 tsp. lime juice
- A pinch of salt and black pepper
- 2 tbsp. coconut milk

>>> Directions:

1. In a blender, combine all the ingredients, pulse well and transfer to a ramekin. Put the ramekin in your air fryer's basket and cook at 350 degrees F for 8 minutes. Serve as a party dip.

Baked Tortillas

Servings: 4   Cooking Time: 30 Mins.

>>> Ingredients:

- 1 large head of cauliflower divided into florets.
- 4 large eggs
- 2 garlic cloves (minced)
- 1 ½ tsp herbs (whatever your favorite is - basil, oregano, thyme)
- ½ tsp salt

>>> Directions:

1. Preheat your fryer to 375°F/190°C.
2. Put parchment paper on two baking sheets.
3. In a food processor, break down the cauliflower into rice.
4. Add ¼ C. water and the riced cauliflower to a saucepan.
5. Cook on a medium high heat until tender for 10 minutes. Drain.
6. Dry with a clean kitchen towel.
7. Mix the cauliflower, eggs, garlic, herbs and salt.
8. Make 4 thin circles on the parchment paper.
9. Bake for 20 minutes, until dry.

Cauliflower Bombs With Sweet & Sour Sauce

Servings: 4   Cooking Time: 25 Mins.

>>> Ingredients:

- Cauliflower Bombs:
- 1/2 lb. cauliflower
- 2 oz. Ricotta cheese
- 1/3 C. Swiss cheese
- 1 egg
- 1 tbsp. Italian seasoning mix
- Sweet & Sour Sauce:
- 1 red bell pepper, jarred
- 1 clove garlic, minced
- 1 tsp. sherry vinegar
- 1 tbsp. tomato puree
- 2 tbsp. olive oil
- Salt and black pepper, to taste

>>> Directions:

1. Blanch the cauliflower in salted boiling water about 3 to 4 Mins. until al dente. Drain well and pulse in a food processor.
2. Add the remaining ingredients for the cauliflower bombs; mix to combine well.
3. Bake in the preheated Air Fryer at 375 degrees F for 16 minutes, shaking halfway through the cooking time.
4. In the meantime, pulse all ingredients for the sauce in your food processor until combined. Season to taste. Serve the cauliflower bombs with the Sweet & Sour Sauce on the side. Bon appétit!

Green Beans And Mushroom Casserole

Servings: 6

Cooking Time: 12 Mins.

>>> Ingredients:

- 24 oz. fresh green beans, trimmed
- 2 C. fresh button mushrooms, sliced
- 1/3 C. French fried onions
- 3 tbsp. olive oil
- 2 tbsp. fresh lemon juice
- 1 tsp. ground sage
- 1 tsp. garlic powder
- 1 tsp. onion powder
- Salt and black pepper, to taste

>>> Directions:

1. Preheat the Air fryer to 400F and grease an Air fryer basket.
2. Mix the green beans, mushrooms, oil, lemon juice, sage, and spices in a bowl and toss to coat well.
3. Arrange the green beans mixture into the Air fryer basket and cook for about 12 minutes.
4. Dish out in a serving dish and top with fried onions to serve.

Veggie Meatballs

>>> Ingredients:

- 2 tbsp soy sauce
- 1 tbsp flax meal
- 2 C. cooked chickpeas
- ½ C. sweet onion, diced
- ½ C. grated carrots
- ½ C. roasted cashews
- Juice of 1 lemon
- ½ tsp turmeric
- 1 tsp cumin
- 1 tsp garlic powder
- 1 C. rolled oats

>>> Directions:

1. Combine oil, onions, and carrots into a baking dish and cook in the air fryer for 6 Mins. at 350 F.

2. Meanwhile, ground the oats and cashews in a food processor. Place them in a large bowl. Process the chickpeas with the lemon juice and soy sauce, until smooth. Add them to the bowl as well.

3. Add onions and carrots to the chickpeas. Stir in the remaining ingredients; mix well. Make meatballs out of the mixture. Increase the temperature to 370 F and cook for 12 minutes, shaking once.

Spicy Braised Vegetables

Servings: 4   Cooking Time: 25 Mins.

>>> Ingredients:

- 1 large-sized zucchini, sliced
- 1 Serrano pepper, deveined and thinly sliced
- 2 bell peppers, deveined and thinly sliced
- 1 celery stalk, cut into matchsticks
- 1/4 C. olive oil
- 1/2 tsp. porcini powder
- 1/4 tsp. mustard powder
- 1/2 tsp. fennel seeds
- 1 tbsp. garlic powder
- 1/2 tsp. fine sea salt
- 1/4 tsp. ground black pepper
- 1/2 C. tomato puree

>>> Directions:

1. Place the sweet potatoes, zucchini, peppers, and the carrot into the Air Fryer cooking basket.
2. Drizzle with olive oil and toss to coat; cook in the preheated Air Fryer at 350 degrees F for 15 minutes.
3. While the vegetables are cooking, prepare the sauce by thoroughly whisking the other ingredients, without the tomato ketchup. Lightly grease a baking dish that fits into your machine.
4. Transfer cooked vegetables to the prepared baking dish; add the sauce and toss to coat well.
5. Turn the Air Fryer to 390 degrees F and cook the vegetables for 5 more minutes. Bon appétit!

Broccoli With Olives

Servings: 4   Cooking Time: 19 Mins.

>>> Ingredients:

- 2 lb. broccoli, stemmed and cut into 1-inch florets
- 1/3 C. Kalamata olives, halved and pitted
- ¼ C. Parmesan cheese, grated
- 2 tbsp. olive oil
- Salt and ground black pepper, as required
- 2 tsp. fresh lemon zest, grated

>>> Directions:

1. Preheat the Air fryer to 400F and grease an Air fryer basket.
2. Boil the broccoli for about 4 Mins. and drain well.
3. Mix broccoli, oil, salt, and black pepper in a bowl and toss to coat well.
4. Arrange broccoli into the Air fryer basket and cook for about 15 minutes.
5. Stir in the olives, lemon zest and cheese and dish out to serve.

Zucchini Garlic-sour Cream Bake

Servings: 5   Cooking Time: 20 Mins.

>>> Ingredients:

- 1 (8 ounce) package cream cheese, softened
- 1 C. sour cream
- 1 large zucchini, cut lengthwise then in half
- 1 tbsp. minced garlic
- 1/4 C. grated Parmesan cheese
- paprika to taste

>>> Directions:

1. Lightly grease baking pan of air fryer with cooking spray.
2. Place zucchini slices in a single layer in pan.
3. In a bowl whisk well, remaining Ingredients except for paprika. Spread on top of zucchini slices. Sprinkle paprika.
4. Cover pan with foil.
5. For 10 minutes, cook on 390oF.
6. Remove foil and cook for 10 Mins. at 330oF.
7. Serve and enjoy.

Open-faced Vegan Flatbread-wich

Servings: 4   Cooking Time: 25 Mins.

>>> Ingredients:

- 1 can chickpeas, drained and rinsed
- 1 medium-sized head of cauliflower, cut into florets
- 1 tbsp. extra-virgin olive oil
- 2 ripe avocados, mashed
- 2 tbsp. lemon juice
- 4 flatbreads, toasted
- salt and pepper to taste

>>> Directions:

1. Preheat the air fryer to 4250F.
2. In a mixing bowl, combine the cauliflower, chickpeas, olive oil, and lemon juice. Season with salt and pepper to taste.
3. Place inside the air fryer basket and cook for 25 minutes.
4. Once cooked, place on half of the flatbread and add avocado mash.
5. Season with more salt and pepper to taste.
6. Serve with hot sauce.

Pesto Tomatoes

>>> Ingredients:

- For Pesto:
- ½ C. plus 1 tbsp. olive oil, divided
- 3 tbsp. pine nuts
- Salt, to taste
- ½ C. fresh basil, chopped
- ½ C. fresh parsley, chopped
- 1 garlic clove, chopped
- ½ C. Parmesan cheese, grated
- For Tomatoes:
- 2 heirloom tomatoes, cut into ½ inch thick slices
- 8 oz. feta cheese, cut into ½ inch thick slices.
- ½ C. red onions, thinly sliced
- 1 tbsp. olive oil
- Salt, to taste

>>> Directions:

1. Set the temperature of air fryer to 390 degrees F. Grease an air fryer basket.
2. In a bowl, mix together one tbsp. of oil, pine nuts and pinch of salt.
3. Arrange pine nuts into the prepared air fryer basket.
4. Air fry for about 1-2 minutes.
5. Remove from air fryer and transfer the pine nuts onto a paper towel-lined plate.
6. In a food processor, add the toasted pine nuts, fresh herbs, garlic, Parmesan, and salt and pulse until just combined.
7. While motor is running, slowly add the remaining oil and pulse until smooth.
8. Transfer into a bowl, covered and refrigerate until serving.
9. Spread about one tbsp. of pesto onto each tomato slice.
10. Top each tomato slice with one feta and onion slice and drizzle with oil.
11. Arrange tomato slices into the prepared air fryer basket in a single layer.
12. Air fry for about 12-14 minutes.
13. Remove from air fryer and transfer the tomato slices onto serving plates.
14. Sprinkle with a little salt and serve with the remaining pesto.

Potato Filled Bread Rolls

Servings: 4

Cooking Time: 25 Mins.

>>> Ingredients:

- 5 large potatoes, boiled and mashed
- ½ tsp turmeric
- 2 green chilies, deseeded and chopped
- 1 medium onion, finely chopped
- ½ tsp mustard seeds
- 1 tbsp olive oil
- 2 sprigs curry leaf
- Salt to taste

>>> Directions:

1. Preheat air fryer to 350 F.
2. Combine olive oil, onion, curry leaves, and mustard seed in a baking dish. Place in the air fryer basket and cook for 5 minutes. Mix the onion mixture with the mashed potatoes, chilies, turmeric, and salt.
3. Divide the mixture into 8 equal pieces. Trim the sides of the bread, and wet with some water. Make sure to get rid of the excess water. Take one wet bread slice in your palm and place one of the potato pieces in the center. Roll the bread over the filling, sealing the edges. Place the rolls onto a prepared baking dish, and air fry for 12 minutes.

Vegetable & Side Dishes

Balsamic Garlic Kale

Servings: 6 Cooking Time: 12 Mins.

>>> Ingredients:

- 2 tbsp. olive oil
- 3 garlic cloves, minced
- 2 and ½ lb. kale leaves
- Salt and black pepper to the taste
- 2 tbsp. balsamic vinegar

>>> Directions:

1. In a pan that fits the air fryer, combine all the ingredients and toss. Put the pan in your air fryer and cook at 300 degrees F for 12 minutes. Divide between plates and serve.

Creamy Potatoes Dish

Servings: 4 Cooking Time: 30 Mins.

>>> Ingredients:

- 1 ½ lbs. potatoes; peeled and cubed
- 2 tbsp. olive oil
- 1 tbsp. hot paprika
- 1 C. Greek yogurt
- Salt and black pepper to the taste

>>> Directions:

1. Put potatoes in a bowl; add water to cover, leave aside for 10 minutes; drain, pat dry them, transfer to another bowl; add salt, pepper, paprika and half of the oil and toss them well.
2. Put potatoes in your air fryer's basket and cook at 360 °F, for 20 minutes.
3. In a bowl; mix yogurt with salt, pepper and the rest of the oil and whisk. Divide potatoes on plates, drizzle yogurt dressing all over; toss them and serve as a side dish.

Rainbow Vegetable And Parmesan Croquettes

Servings: 4   Cooking Time: 40 Mins.

>>> Ingredients:

- 1 lb. potatoes, peeled
- 4 tbsp. milk
- 2 tbsp. butter
- Salt and black pepper, to taste
- 1/2 tsp. cayenne pepper
- 1/2 C. mushrooms, chopped
- 1/4 C. broccoli, chopped
- 1 carrot, grated
- 1 clove garlic, minced
- 3 tbsp. scallions, minced
- 2 tbsp. olive oil
- 1/2 C. all-purpose flour
- 2 eggs
- 1/2 C. panko bread crumbs
- 1/2 C. parmesan cheese, grated

>>> Directions:

1. In a large saucepan, boil the potatoes for 17 to 20 minutes. Drain the potatoes and mash with the milk, butter, salt, black pepper, and cayenne pepper.
2. Add the mushrooms, broccoli, carrots, garlic, scallions, and olive oil; stir to combine well. Shape the mixture into patties.
3. In a shallow bowl, place the flour; beat the eggs in another bowl; in a third bowl, combine the breadcrumbs with the parmesan cheese.
4. Dip each patty into the flour, followed by the eggs, and then the breadcrumb mixture; press to adhere.
5. Cook in the preheated Air Fryer at 375 degrees F for 16 minutes, shaking halfway through the cooking time. Bon appétit!

Cauliflower Rice

Servings: 3

Cooking Time: 12 Mins.

>>> Ingredients:

- 1 cauliflower head, cut into florets
- 2 tbsp olive oil
- 2 garlic cloves, chopped
- 1 tomato, chopped
- 1 onion, chopped
- 2 tbsp tomato paste
- 1 tsp white pepper
- 1 tsp pepper
- 1 tbsp dried thyme
- 2 chilies, chopped
- 1/2 tsp salt

>>> Directions:

1. Preheat the air fryer to 370 F.
2. Add cauliflower florets into the food processor and process until it looks like rice.
3. Stir in tomato paste, tomatoes, and spices and mix well.
4. Add cauliflower mixture into the air fryer baking pan and drizzle with olive oil.
5. Place pan in the air fryer and cook for 12 minutes.
6. Serve and enjoy.

Awesome Cheese Sticks

>>> Ingredients:

- 12 sticks mozzarella cheese
- ¼ C. flour
- 2 C. breadcrumbs
- 2 whole eggs
- ¼ C. Parmesan cheese, grated

>>> Directions:

1. Preheat air fryer to 350 F. Pour breadcrumbs in a bowl. Beat the eggs in a separate bowl. In a third bowl, mix Parmesan and flour. Dip each cheese stick the in flour mixture, then in eggs and finally in breadcrumbs. Put in air fryer's basket and cook for 7 minutes, turning once.

Goat Cheese Cauliflower And Bacon

>>> Ingredients:

- 8 C. cauliflower florets, roughly chopped
- 4 bacon strips, chopped
- Salt and black pepper to the taste
- ½ C. spring onions, chopped
- 1 tbsp. garlic, minced
- 10 oz. goat cheese, crumbled
- ¼ C. soft cream cheese
- Cooking spray

>>> Directions:

1. Grease a baking pan that fits the air fryer with the cooking spray and mix all the ingredients except the goat cheese into the pan. Sprinkle the cheese on top, introduce the pan in the machine and cook at 400 degrees F for 20 minutes. Divide between plates and serve as a side dish.

Shallots Almonds Green Beans

Servings: 6 Cooking Time: 15 Mins.

>>> Ingredients:

- 🌀 1/4 C. almonds, toasted
- 🌀 1 1/2 lbs green beans, trimmed and steamed
- 🌀 2 tbsp olive oil
- 🌀 1/2 lb shallots, chopped
- 🌀 Pepper
- 🌀 Salt

>>> Directions:

1. Add all ingredients into the large bowl and toss well.
2. Transfer green bean mixture into the air fryer basket and cook at 400 F for 15 minutes.
3. Serve and enjoy.

Coriander Leeks

Servings: 6   Cooking Time: 10 Mins.

>>> Ingredients:

- 🌀 10 oz leek, chopped
- 🌀 2 tbsp. ricotta
- 🌀 1 tbsp. butter, melted
- 🌀 1 tsp. ground coriander
- 🌀 ¼ tsp. salt

>>> Directions:

1. Sprinkle the leek with salt and ground coriander and transfer in the air fryer. Add butter and gently stir the ingredients. After this, cook the leek for 5 Mins. at 375F. Stir the vegetables well and add ricotta. Cook the meal for 5 Mins. more. Serve the cooked leek with ricotta gravy.

Other Air Fryer Recipes

Fruit Skewers With A Greek Flair

>>> Ingredients:

- 6 strawberries, halved
- 1 banana, peeled and sliced
- 1/4 pineapple, peeled and cubed
- 1 tsp. fresh lemon juice
- 1/4 C. Greek-Style yoghurt, optional
- 2 tbsp. honey
- 1 tsp. vanilla

>>> Directions:

1. Toss the fruits with lemon juice in a mixing dish. Tread the fruit pieces on skewers.
2. Cook at 340 degrees F for 5 minutes.
3. Meanwhile, whisk the Greek yogurt with the honey and vanilla. Serve the fruit skewers with the Greek sauce on the side. Bon appétit!

Scrambled Egg Muffins With Cheese

>>> Ingredients:

- 6 oz. smoked turkey sausage, chopped
- 6 eggs, lightly beaten
- 2 tbsp. shallots, finely chopped
- 2 garlic cloves, minced
- Sea salt and ground black pepper, to taste
- 1 tsp. cayenne pepper
- 6 oz. Monterey Jack cheese, shredded

>>> Directions:

1. Simply combine the sausage, eggs, shallots, garlic, salt, black pepper, and cayenne pepper in a mixing dish. Mix to combine well.
2. Spoon the mixture into 6 standard-size muffin C. with paper liners.
3. Bake in the preheated Air Fryer at 340 degrees F for 8 minutes. Top with the cheese and bake an additional 8 minutes. Enjoy!

Cranberry Cornbread Muffins

Servings: 4   Cooking Time: 35 Mins.

>>> Ingredients:

- 3/4 C. all-purpose flour
- 3/4 C. cornmeal
- 1 tsp. baking powder
- 1/2 tsp. baking soda
- 1/2 tsp. salt
- 3 tbsp. honey
- 1 egg, well whisked
- 1/4 C. olive oil
- 3/4 C. milk
- 1/2 C. fresh cranberries, roughly chopped

>>> Directions:

1. In a mixing dish, thoroughly combine the flour, cornmeal, baking powder, baking soda, and salt. In a separate bowl, mix the honey, egg, olive oil, and milk.

2. Next, stir the liquid mixture into the dry ingredients; mix to combine well. Fold in the fresh cranberries and stir to combine well.

3. Pour the batter into a lightly greased muffin tin; cover with aluminum foil and poke tiny little holes all over the foil. Now, bake for 15 minutes.

4. Remove the foil and bake for 10 Mins. more. Transfer to a wire rack to cool slightly before cutting and serving. Bon appétit!

Dinner Avocado Chicken Sliders

Servings: 4 Cooking Time: 10 Mins.

>>> Ingredients:

- ½ lb. ground chicken meat
- 4 burger buns
- 1/2 C. Romaine lettuce, loosely packed
- ½ tsp. dried parsley flakes
- 1/3 tsp. mustard seeds
- 1 tsp. onion powder
- 1 ripe fresh avocado, mashed
- 1 tsp. garlic powder
- 1 ½ tbsp. extra-virgin olive oil
- 1 cloves garlic, minced
- Nonstick cooking spray
- Salt and cracked black pepper (peppercorns, to taste

>>> Directions:

1. Firstly, spritz an air fryer cooking basket with a nonstick cooking spray.
2. Mix ground chicken meat, mustard seeds, garlic powder, onion powder, parsley, salt, and black pepper until everything is thoroughly combined. Make sure not to overwork the meat to avoid tough chicken burgers.
3. Shape the meat mixture into patties and roll them in breadcrumbs; transfer your burgers to the prepared cooking basket. Brush the patties with the cooking spray.
4. Air-fry at 355 F for 9 minutes, working in batches. Slice burger buns into halves. In the meantime, combine olive oil with mashed avocado and pressed garlic.
5. To finish, lay Romaine lettuce and avocado spread on bun bottoms; now, add burgers and bun tops. Bon appétit!

Mother's Day Pudding

Servings: 6　　　Cooking Time: 45 Mins.

>>> Ingredients:

- 1 lb. French baguette bread, cubed
- 4 eggs, beaten
- 1/4 C. chocolate liqueur
- 1 C. granulated sugar
- 2 tbsp. honey
- 2 C. whole milk
- 1/2 C. heavy cream
- 1 tsp. vanilla extract
- 1/4 tsp. ground cloves
- 2 oz. milk chocolate chips

>>> Directions:

1. Place the bread cubes in a lightly greased baking dish. In a mixing bowl, thoroughly combine the eggs, chocolate liqueur, sugar, honey, milk, heavy cream, vanilla, and ground cloves.
2. Pour the custard over the bread cubes. Scatter the milk chocolate chips over the top of your bread pudding.
3. Let stand for 30 minutes, occasionally pressing with a wide spatula to submerge.
4. Cook in the preheated Air Fryer at 370 degrees F degrees for 7 minutes; check to ensure even cooking and cook an additional 5 to 6 minutes. Bon appétit!

Crunch-crunch Party Mix

Servings: 8   Cooking Time: 25 Mins.

>>> Ingredients:

- 1 C. whole-grain Rice Chex
- 2 C. cheese squares
- 1 C. pistachios
- 1/2 C. almonds
- 1 C. cheddar-flavored mini pretzel twists
- 2 tbsp. butter, melted
- 1/4 C. poppy seeds
- 1/2 C. sunflower seeds
- 1 tbsp. coarse sea salt
- 1 tbsp. garlic powder
- 1 tbsp. paprika

>>> Directions:

1. Mix all ingredients in a large bowl. Toss to combine well.
2. Place in a single layer in the parchment-lined cooking basket.
3. Bake in the preheated Air Fryer at 310 degrees F for 13 to 16 minutes. Allow it to cool completely before serving.
4. Store in an airtight container for up to 3 months. Bon appétit!

Celery Fries With Harissa Mayo

Servings: 3   Cooking Time: 30 Mins.

>>> Ingredients:

- 1/2 lb. celery root
- 2 tbsp. olive oil
- Sea salt and ground black pepper, to taste
- Harissa Mayo
- 1/4 C. mayonnaise
- 2 tbsp. sour cream
- 1/2 tbsp. harissa paste
- 1/4 tsp. ground cumin
- Salt, to taste

>>> Directions:

1. Cut the celery root into desired size and shape.
2. Then, preheat your Air Fryer to 400 degrees F. Now, spritz the Air Fryer basket with cooking spray.
3. Toss the celery fries with the olive oil, salt, and black pepper. Bake in the preheated Air Fryer for 25 to 30 minutes, turning them over every 10 Mins. to promote even cooking.
4. Meanwhile, mix all ingredients for the harissa mayo. Place in your refrigerator until ready to serve. Bon appétit!

Baked Eggs With Linguica Sausage

Servings: 2   Cooking Time: 18 Mins.

>>> Ingredients:

- 1/2 C. Cheddar cheese, shredded
- 4 eggs
- 2 oz. Linguica (Portuguese pork sausage), chopped
- 1/2 onion, peeled and chopped
- 2 tbsp. olive oil
- 1/2 tsp. rosemary, chopped
- ½ tsp. marjoram
- 1/4 C. sour cream
- Sea salt and freshly ground black pepper, to taste
- ½ tsp. fresh sage, chopped

>>> Directions:

1. Lightly grease 2 oven safe ramekins with olive oil. Now, divide the sausage and onions among these ramekins.
2. Crack an egg into each ramekin; add the remaining items, minus the cheese. Air-fry at 355 degrees F approximately 13 minutes.
3. Immediately top with Cheddar cheese, serve, and enjoy.

Printed in Great Britain
by Amazon

13042069R00045